God of Love

Susan Hardwick

First published in 1998 by
KEVIN MAYHEW LTD
Rattlesden
Bury St Edmunds
Suffolk IP30 0SZ

ISBN 1 84003 173 5
Catalogue No 1500182

0 1 2 3 4 5 6 7 8 9

Cover design by Jaquetta Sergeant
Edited by Katherine Laidler
Typesetting by Louise Selfe
Printed and bound in Great Britain

CONTENTS

ACKNOWLEDGEMENTS

Bible quotations are taken from:

– The Holy Bible, *New International Version*, © Copyright 1973, 1978, 1984 by International Bible Society, published by Hodder and Stoughton Ltd. All rights reserved. 'NIV' is a registered trademark of International Bible Society. UK trademark number 1448790.

– *The New Jerusalem Bible* published and © Copyright 1985 by Darton Longman and Todd Ltd and Doubleday and Co Inc. and used by permission of the publisher.

– *The Message* © Copyright by Eugene H. Peterson, 1993, 1994, 1995, 1996, 1997. Used by permission of NavPress Publishing Group.

The stories from *Taking Flight* by Anthony de Mello are reproduced by kind permission of Gujarat Sahitya Prakash, Anand, Gujarat, 388 001 India.

THE FIRST WORD

From darkness through the dawn to daylight, from our experiences of loneliness through to love, God's constancy, commitment and love never fail. We may not always recognise him, but he is there.

Using prayers, stories, reflections and Bible passages, this little book reflects on that truth.

Most of our opposite experiences are two sides of the same coin: one emphasises the other, as do darkness and light, night and day. Just as night and day are integral to the rhythm of Creation, so are our negative and positive experiences integral to our human condition.

The secret of joyful, fearless living, then, is to be as ready to embrace the one as the other, in confidence and trust and expectation that, when we are in the difficult, hard times, the dawn will finally break upon the night sky and dispel the darkness.

The title CROSS+WORDS reflects the truth that, through our prayer and Christ's Cross, we are linked to the healing touch of Jesus upon and within our lives.

SUSAN HARDWICK

PRAYERS

Don't fret or worry. Instead of worrying, pray. Let petitions and praises shape your worries into prayers, letting God know your concerns. Before you know it, a sense of God's wholeness, everything coming together for good, will come and settle you down. It's wonderful what happens when Christ displaces worry at the centre of your life.
Philippians 4:5b-7 (The Message)

DARK: LONELY

This aching space

O God!
I'm just *so* lonely.
Please take away this aching space.
Please send someone to care.
Please help me.
Amen.

Reach out to me

Jesus,
loneliness seems to have put
a shell around me
that even you can't break through.
Yet, I believe you are there,
in the dark.
Even if I can't reach out to you
at this moment in time,
I know you are reaching out to me.
Stay close.
Don't leave me alone.
I need you.
Amen.

Open my eyes, my heart

Jesus,
I walked past that sign today,
declaring there were
'people who needed love'.
How true.
I know – because I'm one of them.
I have so much love to give, too,
but no one who appears to want it.
How sad and ironic it is

that there is this huge mismatch of needs.
Open my eyes to possibilities
beyond those that I have tried.
Open my heart to new ways
of seeing things.
Open the gateway of my life,
so people may walk through.
Amen.

Filling the empty space with over-activity

Dear God,
to many people I guess I appear
fulfilled and very busy.
But there's a hole at the centre
of my life labelled 'lonely'.

When the activity stops,
and I'm on my own once more,
its presence is even more apparent.
Then the temptation is
to speed up my life yet another notch
and pack in even more.
Yet the hole remains
– and it's very, very painful.

Give me the courage I need
to turn around and to face it:
to look inward,
rather than always resolutely outward.
Give me the wisdom
to understand where
and what
changes are needed
– and then the determination
to do something about it.
Amen.

So much love needed

So many lonely people.
So much love needed.
You saw that,
Jesus.
You put aside your own needs
and did what you could
to lighten the darkness
with your love.
Help me to be more like you.
Amen.

Dawn: Befriended

I'm on the way!

Dear God,
the dawn has come,
lighting up the night sky.
From loneliness to love;
my journey has begun.
I'm on the way!
Thank you!
Amen.

A cosy cocoon?

Jesus,
I've not beaten it yet.
One thing, though, I have realised
is that loneliness *can* become a cosy
    cocoon,
which prevents you from engaging
with the isolation and pain of others.

But when I find myself retreating
behind that protective screen I
– or, in reality, is it you? –
make myself turn right round
and walk back into the world once more.

Thank you for your gentle persuasion
that encourages
but *never* coerces.
Amen.

A new way of seeing

Dear God,
I prayed for things to be different;
for a new way of seeing –
and you have answered my prayer.

The gateway to my life
has begun to swing open –
creaking and protesting
from too-long lack of use.
Now I am beginning to venture out –
and I am also letting people in.

And I wonder,
did some of the fault
lie with me all along?
Was I too absorbed in my own pain
to notice that of others?
Thank you for turning my heart
inside out.
Help me to build
on what you have begun.
Amen.

Of value, and valued

Jesus,
in the depths of the night,
I cried out to you.
You took my hand
and led me
towards the dawning east.

In my darkest hours
of deepest loneliness,
you befriended me.
You have made me feel
lovable once more.

In my reflection,
mirrored in your love,
I see myself now
as of value,
and valued.
If *you* can love me,
why not others, too?

Thank you
for giving me back
my sense of self-worth.
Amen.

DAY: LOVE

Transformation

Jesus,
from loneliness to love:
you have turned my sighs
into song.
My darkness has transformed
into bright day
in the light of your tender care.
Amen.

Love changes everything

O God,
most holy and tender God,
how true it is
– I never knew it properly until now –
that love changes *everything*.
Little by little,
I've allowed your love
to seep into my soul.
Then, when your work was complete,
it burst into full flower,
and your true glory was revealed.
My whole world has been lit up.
Now I see your beauty
where formerly I saw none.
To know myself as so totally loved,
is truly the greatest
of heavenly blessings.
Amen.

All is grace

Why me?
Why not, I suppose.
But still I cannot believe it.
What *have* I done to deserve it?
Was it my struggles you honoured
by letting me know your love in this way?

It must have been;
for there are so many others
more worthy than me
to receive such a blessing.

All is grace.
All is grace.
Thank you, Lord.
Thank you.
Amen.

REFLECTIONS

O God,
without you,
nothing makes sense.
Psalm 16:1b (The Message)

A TALE OF LOVE

A little girl was dying of a disease from which her eight-year-old brother had recovered some time before.

The doctor said to the boy, 'Only a transfusion of your blood will save the life of your sister. Will you give her your blood?'

The eyes of the boy widened in fear. He hesitated for a while, then finally said, 'OK. Yes. I'll do it.'

An hour after the transfusion was completed the boy asked hesitantly, 'Doctor – when will I die?'

It was only then that the doctor understood the fear that had seized the child. The young boy had thought that, in giving his blood, he was giving his life for his sister.

Jesus said,
'My command is this:
Love each other as I have loved you.
Greater love has no one than this,
that he lay down his life for his friends.'
John 15:12, 13 (NIV)

ANOTHER TALE OF LOVE

A very wise old man, revered by many as a guru, asked his disciples how they could tell when the night had ended and the day begun.

One said, 'When you see an animal in the distance and can tell whether it is a cow or a horse.'

'No,' said the guru.

'When you look at a tree in the distance and can tell if it is an apple or a pear tree,' ventured another.

'Wrong again,' said the guru.

'Well, then, what is it?' asked his disciples.

'When you look into the face of any woman and recognise in her your sister; when you look into the face of any man and recognise your brother in him. If you cannot do this, no matter what time it is by the sun, it is still night.'

(Both stories from *Taking Flight*, by Anthony de Mello SJ)

Reflection

Let's not just talk about love;
let's practise real love.
This is the only way we'll know we're living
truly,
living in God's reality.
It's also the way to shut down debilitating
self-criticism,
even when there is something to it.
For God is greater than our worried hearts
and knows more about us than we do
ourselves.
1 John 3:18-20 (The Message)

More has been written about love than anything else, it would seem. And yet there have probably never been more people feeling lonely and unloved than now.

As families split and divide, then split and divide again, the traditional structures and frameworks and wider context against which people have tradition-ally defined their identity and picture of themselves are often no longer there. An empty space now surrounds many people like a cocoon.

The question, 'Who am I?' never gets a proper answer and so, when the crowd, or busyness, does not fill the gap there is an emptiness, a void, into which loneliness can so easily creep.

There is a world of difference between being alone and being lonely. Loneliness can be at its most acute when surrounded by other people.

Jesus knew about aloneness, which he often sought as a balance from the pressing crowds, and in order to be with the Father.

> The news about Jesus spread,
> so that crowds of people came to hear him
> and to be healed of their sicknesses.
> But Jesus often withdrew to lonely places
> and prayed.
> *Luke 5:15, 16 (NIV)*

However, he must have known all about loneliness, too. People, even his closest friends and his family, so often did not understand him and his mission.

The disciples did not, at the time, understand the significance of what he did at the Last Supper; they went to sleep instead of keeping him company in the Garden of Gethsemane.

And Jesus knew all about utter loneliness and a sense of rejection when he thought that God had deserted him as he hung on the Cross.

So, no one better understands our loneliness than does Jesus, for he was there first. Through his Spirit, he is our nearest, our dearest, companion – closer to us than we are to ourselves. His tender love is beyond description, and his constancy beyond our human understanding, surrounding us and dwelling within us, soothing away our tears and sharing in our joy.

In our success-orientated world, we are often seduced into thinking that, as long as we can achieve certain things, our lives will be fine. We will be happy. People will value and love us for what we have achieved.

However, too often we find that achievement and success in life do not, in fact, give us these things; rather, they undermine our security, and generate anxiety. A cycle of need, to keep proving ourselves in order to gain the approval which we seek, is set in motion. And, if we don't get it in sufficient quantity, further anxiety and loneliness and emptiness are generated.

Success tells me my achievements are fine. But love tells me that *I* am fine.

Beethoven, one of the most famous composers ever, was a very lonely and unhappy man because people appreciated and valued his music, but not him as a person and for his own sake.

Love, the pearl beyond price, cannot be bought. To know ourselves to be loved for ourselves is one of the greatest gifts we can be given.

Jesus, though, in the way he so often does, challenges us to go one stage further. To love others is the most important thing, he declares. But you must also accept and love others, regardless of how they feel about you:

> 'But I tell you who hear me:
> Love your enemies.
> Do good to them.
> Do to others
> as you would have them do to you.
> If you love those who love you,
> what credit is that to you?'
> *Luke 6:31-32a (NIV)*

Real love, Jesus love, is not about inclination; it's about decision and the state of mind which acknowledges that we each have it in our power to choose whom we love and how we love.

Your love for others should not, Jesus says, be dependent upon their love and regard for you. It should be about a state, a condition, of mind and heart which loves because God first loved you. A state of mind and heart which says, because of this I can do no other.

> For this is how God loved the world:
> he gave his only Son,
> so that everyone who believes in him
> may not perish,
> but may have eternal life.
> *John 3:16 (NJB)*

Just one verse of twenty-eight words and packed with explosive meaning, sums up the Christian message.

This message was the focus of all that Jesus did.

If we *all* took Jesus' command to love seriously, just imagine what power would be released into the world; it would be a tidal wave sweeping everyone and everything before it.

However, like every change, it needs to begin with the individual saying not 'This is what *others* should do', but 'This is what *I* shall do'.

To know yourself to be loved dispels the darkness and makes the sun shine upon you.

To know how to love another in a way that sets that person free to be his or her best self is to make the Son shine within you.

The Way of Love

So, no matter what I say, what I believe,
what I do, I'm bankrupt without love.
    Love never gives up.
    Love cares more for others than for self.
    Love doesn't want what it doesn't have.
    Love doesn't strut.
    Doesn't have a swelled head.
    Doesn't force itself on others.
    Isn't always 'me first'.
    Doesn't fly off the handle.
    Doesn't keep score of the sins of others.
    Doesn't revel when others grovel.
    Takes pleasure in the flowering of the truth.
    Puts up with anything.
    Trusts God always.
    Always looks for the best.
    Never looks back.
    But keeps going to the end.

    Love never dies.

We have three things to do to lead us
toward God. Trust steadily in him, hope
unswervingly, love extravagantly. And the
best of the three is love.
1 Corinthians 13 (The Message, adapted)

WORDS FROM SCRIPTURE

Jesus addressed the crowds, using this story:
   'A farmer went out to sow his seed. Some of it fell on the road; it was trampled down and the birds ate it. Other seed fell in the gravel; it sprouted, but withered because it didn't have good roots. Other seed fell in the weeds; the weeds grew with it and strangled it. Other seed fell in rich earth and produced a bumper crop . . .

   This is the meaning of the parable:
   the seed is the Word of God.'
   Luke 8:5-8, 11 (The Message)

THE OLD TESTAMENT

In your unfailing love you will lead
the people you have redeemed.
In your strength you will guide them
to your holy dwelling.
Exodus 15:13 (NIV)

Do not seek revenge or bear a grudge
against one of your people,
but love your neighbour as yourself.
I am the Lord.
Leviticus 19:18 (NIV)

Love the Lord your God with all your heart
and with all your soul and with all your
    strength . . .
Know that the Lord your God is the faithful
    God,
keeping his covenant of love to a thousand
    generations
of those who love him and keep his
    commands.
Deuteronomy 6:5; 7:9 (NIV)

But I trust in your unfailing love.
Psalm 13:5a (NIV)

I love you, O Lord, my strength.
The Lord is my rock, my fortress
and my deliverer;
my God is my rock, in whom I take refuge.
Psalm 18:1, 2a (NIV)

Surely goodness and love will follow me
all the days of my life,
and I will dwell in the house of the Lord
for ever.
Psalm 23:6 (NIV)

The Lord loves righteousness and justice;
the earth is full of his unfailing love.
Psalm 33:5 (NIV)

For great is your love, reaching to the heavens.
Psalm 57:10a (NIV)

Hatred provokes disputes,
but love excuses all offences.
Proverbs 10:12 (NJB)

Since you are precious and honoured in my
    sight,
and because I love you . . .
Isaiah 43:4a (NIV)

The Lord said, 'I have loved you
with an everlasting love.'
Jeremiah 31:3a (NIV)

And what does the Lord require of you?
To act justly and to love mercy
and to walk humbly with your God.
Micah 6:8b (NIV)

THE NEW TESTAMENT

A voice from the cloud said,
'This is my Son, whom I love;
with him I am well pleased.
Listen to him!'
Matthew 17:5b (NIV)

One of those listening asked Jesus,
'Of all the commandments,
which is the most important?'
Jesus said,
'Love the Lord your God with all your heart
and with all your soul and with all your mind
and with all your strength.
The second is this:
Love your neighbour as yourself.
There is no commandment greater than these.'
Mark 12:28b-31 (NIV)

It was just before the Passover Feast.
Jesus knew that the time had come for him
to leave this world and go to the Father.
Having loved his own who were in the world,
he now showed them the full extent of his
   love.
John 13:1 (NIV)

Jesus said,
'A new command I give you: Love one another.
As I have loved you,
so you must love one another.'
John 13:34 (NIV)

Jesus said,
'If you love me you will obey what I command.'
John 14:15 (NIV)

Jesus said,
'As the Father has loved me,
so have I loved you.
Now remain in my love.'
John 15:9 (NIV)

God has poured out his love into our hearts
by the Holy Spirit, whom he has given us.
Romans 5:5b (NIV)

No eye has seen, no ear has heard,
no mind has conceived what God has
    prepared
for those who love him.
1 Corinthians 2:9 (NIV)

But the fruit of the Spirit is love, joy, peace . . .
Galatians 5:22a (NIV)

Dear friends, let us love one another,
for love comes from God.
Everyone who loves has been born of God
and knows God. Whoever does not love
does not know God, because God is love . . .
For anyone who does not love their brother
    or sister,
whom they have seen, cannot love God,
whom they have not seen.
1 John 4:7, 8, 20b (NIV, adapted)

There is no fear in love,
but perfect love drives out fear.
1 John 4:18 (NIV)

THE LAST WORD

I am well on my way,
reaching out for Christ,
who has so wondrously reached out for
    me . . .
I've got my eye on the goal
where God is beckoning us onward –
    to Jesus.
I'm off and running,
and I'm not turning back.
So let's keep focused on that goal,
those of us who want everything God has
    for us.
If you have something else in mind,
something less than total commitment,
God will clear your blurred vision –
you'll see it yet!
Now that we're on the right track
let's stay on it.
Don't waver.
Stay on track,
steady in God.
Philippians 3:12-16; 4:1b (The Message)

Jesus said:
'You didn't choose me, remember;
I chose you,
and I put you in the world
to bear fruit,
fruit that won't spoil.'
John 15:16a (The Message)